Jill at the Fa

3. Well, when the children had finished the hoopla game, they looked round for their pup. But they could not find him anywhere. "Have you seen our little dog?" they asked a policeman. "No," said the policeman. "But he can't be far."

4. Patch was not far away! The steps he had gone up led to the top of the helter skelter tower. Just as the children were passing the bottom of it, Patch came whizzing down on a mat. "There's your pup," laughed the policeman.

7. "Oh, my goodness," he gasped. "There is a great big dog looking at me." And he rushed out of the hall of mirrors without realising that he had been looking at himself. Jack and Jill were surprised to see him come racing out.

8. But they guessed what had happened. "You should have waited for us," said Jill. Anyway, they took him back inside and Patch found that every mirror made him look different. He quite enjoyed himself in the end. Funny little pup.

'Published by IPC Magazines Ltd., King's Reach Tower, Stamford Street, London SE1 9LS, England. Sole Agents for Australia and New Zealand: Gordon & Gotch Ltd., South Africa: Central News Agency. Printed in England by Fleetway Printers Gravesend, Kent.' Covers laminated by Olro Coatings Ltd., using Bexphane film

£1.40

An Exciting Day At The Seaside

GREGORY GRASSHOPPER and his friends, Lottie Ladybird, Belinda Butterfly, Mr. Bumble Bee, Wilbur Wasp and Doctor Beetle went to the seaside for the day.

Gregory found a beautiful shell while Doctor Beetle and Lottie danced in the sand.

"I can see a lovely place for us to play," said Belinda, as she flew above the others with Wilbur and Mr. Bumble Bee.

Belinda had seen a stretch of sand with a small rock pool in it.

The little folk rushed to that part of the beach and were soon having a lovely time.

Gregory and Mr. Bumble Bee built a nice sandcastle.

Doctor Beetle found a shell.

"This will make a nice boat for me," he laughed. And then Wilbur found some lolly sticks, two of which made oars for Doctor Beetle's boat. Everyone thought that the seaside was wonderful.

After playing on the beach for a little while, Belinda said, "I think we should start getting our picnic ready. I am feeling hungry."
So the friends set to work finding a nice place to eat. Gregory found an excitingly shaped shell, and right beside it was a flat pebble that would make an ideal table.
Doctor Beetle found some small pebbles to sit on, while Wilbur, Mr. Bumble Bee and Lottie searched for berries and things to eat.
There were lots of seashells to use as plates, and soon the folk were ready to eat their meal.
They were about to start, when Gregory noticed that Doctor Beetle wasn't sitting at the table.
"Where is Doctor Beetle?" he said.
The friends called and called.
But Doctor Beetle did not answer, so they decided to search for him.
They looked inside shells, under stones, in rock pools, but Doctor Beetle was nowhere to be found.

"Where can he have got to?" said Belinda, looking quite worried.
Then Gregory looked out to sea, and said, "I can see him!"

Gregory had spotted Doctor Beetle sitting on a tiny island.

"How did he get there?" said Lottie.

Gregory asked Wilbur to fly out and ask Doctor Beetle.

"While you are gone, we will try and think of a way to rescue him," said Gregory.

So Wilbur flew out to the doctor.

"I wanted to see if my shell boat would float out on the sea," said Doctor Beetle. "But it sank by this island, and now I am stranded."

"Don't worry," said Wilbur. "Help is on the way."

And the little wasp flew back to where Gregory and Mr. Bumble Bee were busy making a boat out of a matchbox.

"We are nearly ready to rescue Doctor Beetle," said Gregory.

Soon the matchbox boat was sailing out to sea with Gregory, Wilbur and Mr. Bumble Bee.

Doctor Beetle jumped for joy when he saw them.

"Hooray, hooray!" he shouted. "Hurry up, I am feeling hungry."

But oh dear! The matchbox was only made out of paper and card and it started to fill up with water, and then it sank.

Luckily it sank near the island and Gregory and Mr. Bumble Bee were able to swim there.

Doctor Beetle helped them ashore.

"Oh dear, we are all stranded now," sighed Doctor Beetle. "And it is all my fault."

The little folk sat feeling rather sorry for themselves.

"Perhaps I could fly and get help," said Wilbur.

But no one could think of who could help them get ashore.

Then Gregory gave a happy shout. "Look, two seahorses are swimming this way," he cheered. "Perhaps they will help us get off this island."

The seahorses said they would help and they found a big shell.

"Get in the shell and we will tow you back to the beach," they told the stranded insects.

Soon the friends were being towed through the sea, back to land.

Belinda and Lottie were glad to see their friends again.

"Thank you for your help," Gregory told the seahorses.

Well, after all that excitement, the little folk were tired. So they had a nap inside a big seashell.

None of them saw a little girl out searching for seashells, and she didn't see those insects when she found that seashell and took it home.

They were all fast asleep inside!

When they woke up, Gregory and his friends were surprised to find themselves in a pretty garden.

There was a pretty pond in the garden. The folk thought it was just like being at the seaside.

In fact they liked it better.

The pond was nice and shallow and Gregory found a water lily leaf to use as a boat.

"I don't think we will get stranded this time," he laughed.

And they didn't!

FRIENDLY PENGUINS

Although penguins are birds, they cannot fly. But in the sea they can swim through the water faster than many fish can swim. Penguins are mainly found near the South Pole but you may see some at a zoo.

When a penguin is looking for a wife, he finds a nice pebble and drops it in front of the penguin of his choice. The big penguin below is called an Emperor Penguin.

Easter Time at the

1. Nellyphant the elephant, Joe the kangaroo and Tiny the giraffe live in the Enchanted House. Their friends, Worm and Bob Robin, live in the garden.One day, they had a surprise.

2. There was a knock-knock on the front door and when Joe opened it, the friends found Felix Fox with a present. "This Easter egg is for you all," said Felix."Thank you" said Joe.

3. The friends felt a bit surprised. Felix is usually a crafty fox. They took the Easter egg indoors and had an even bigger surprise. It was a trick egg and when they opened it a toy jumped out.

7."I wonder what is inside?" said Felix. The friends stood and watched Felix unwrap the parcel. Inside was a lovely chocolate coloured Easter egg. "Ho, ho," laughed Felix.

8. The friends smiled. They had sent the Easter egg to Felix. Then Felix did something rather surprising. "I don't want that Easter egg," he said. "You can have it. You can't trick me!"

9. And he ran off leaving the egg on the ground. He thought that it was a trick egg, you see! But it wasn't a trick egg. It was a real egg, full of chocolate beans. Silly crafty Felix Fox.

Enchanted House

4. Goodness—what a scare it gave them. Felix, who was looking in through the window, chuckled, "Oh, what a funny joke." "We should have known it was a trick," said Tiny.

5. The friends decided to go outside and tell Felix off. But Felix ran away. As he ran down the path, Postman Blackbird flew up. "Wait a moment, Felix," he chirped, "a parcel for you."

6. "A parcel for me?" said Felix in surprise. Nellyphant and the others stood and watched. They knew what was in that parcel you see. Felix took the parcel from Postman Blackbird.

10. "Are you sure you don't want it?" said Joe. Felix said he was sure. "Goody," thought Worm. "I love eating chocolate." Felix expected to hear shrieks of surprise. But he didn't.

11. What a surprise Felix had when he turned and saw the folk eating the chocolate Easter egg. "Oh dear," he sighed. "I think I have been a silly fox." Worm thought it was very funny.

12. But the Enchanted House folk are kind and Nellyphant said he could share the Easter egg too. "I'm sorry I tricked you," said Felix, "I won't do it again." He had learnt—for now!

ERNEST HELPS THE BAKER

1. Ernest is a funny chap who loves to help folk. But usually things go wrong when Ernest tries to help! One morning, Ernest woke up and looked out of the window. He saw Mr. Bun the baker coming up the garden path.

2. "Mr. Bun must get tired having to deliver bread all the time," thought Ernest. "I will help him." He was so eager to help, that he didn't even get dressed. He ran downstairs and outside, snatching the bread basket as he went.

3. "You have a rest," said Ernest. "I will deliver the bread today." And off he raced down the street. It all happened so fast, that Mr. Bun couldn't stop Ernest. And he wasn't very pleased with Ernest either. Just look!

4. Instead of walking up the garden path of each house and carefully putting the bread somewhere nice and clean, or handing it to the customer, Ernest ran down the street, *throwing* the bread at the customers' houses. Silly Ernest!

5. One loaf landed on the ground, another knocked over some milk and another hit a gentleman in the tummy. Mr. Bun raced after Ernest. "Stop, stop, please stop," he shouted. But Ernest was too busy being helpful to hear him.

6. Ernest didn't stop until he had delivered all the bread. "There, haven't I been helpful?" said Ernest. "No you haven't," said Mr. Bun. "My customers are not very pleased—look." Some customers were marching along crossly.

7. You see, all the bread had been spoilt. "Now I shall have to bake some more," said Mr. Bun. "And you can help by doing it for me." So silly Ernest had to go to the bakehouse and work for the rest of the day!

HAROLD HARE

1. It was the day of the Leafy Wood Cross-country race. The Mayor and lots of other folk were waiting at the winning tape to present the prizes. At last Dicky Dormouse heard someone running. It was Harold Hare—he had won.

2. Everyone cheered and the Mayor presented the first prize—a huge box of chocolates. As he was taking the chocolates, Harold noticed the second prize—a yummy cherry cake. "That would be nice for tea," thought Harold.

3. Then Harold had an idea. "If I run fast enough, I could beat the others and win the cake too," he thought. So Harold went racing off along the course. In next to no time, he had caught up with the others and whizzed past.

4. Harold, of course, is a hare, and hares are very fast runners. So he reached the winning post again before any of the others and was awarded the cake. Then Harold noticed the third prize—a bag of Goody Gumdrops!

The Prize Winner

5. Harold loves Goody Gumdrops. So do you know what he did? He took a deep breath and went racing off *again*. This time he had to run very fast indeed, and he only just managed to pass the others and reach the winning tape first!

6. Harold was very pleased with himself. He had won the first, second and third prizes all in one race. Lots of newspaper and film folk wanted to take his picture. So Harold stood with his prizes and posed for them. Dicky was proud too.

7. Then Harold noticed the other runners. They did look sad. There was only the booby prize left, as Harold had won all the other prizes. "I have been selfish," thought Harold. Now, Harold is a kind hare so he called them back.

8. "You can have these prizes," he told them. "I only ran round the track three times for fun. I will have the booby prize." Wasn't that kind? Harold was pleased with the booby prize—it was a bunch of lovely scrunchy carrots!

JACK
The Gentle Giant

ONCE upon a time there was a pretty little village in Happyland where it was very quiet and nothing exciting ever happened. Then one day all the ground began to shake as, thump, thump, thump, big footsteps came towards the village.

"Look," called a little boy. "A giant! Look, look!"

Sure enough, coming straight for the village was a huge giant.

Everyone scurried home as fast as possible and hid in houses, under tables and chairs, and even in baths.

Outside everything went quiet. The giant, who towered over the houses in the village, stood and waited.

Because it was so quiet, a little boy peeked out.

"It is all right," he called. "The giant has gone. I can't see him anywhere."

But the little boy had only looked down the street. If he had looked upwards, he would have seen the giant standing over his house, his feet hidden by other houses in the street.

Folk stopped shaking with fright and came out from their hiding places.

Suddenly a voice called out, a big booming voice, "My name is Jack, and I have come to live in the cave on the hill behind this village."

Everyone stopped in amazement.

But before anyone could run away and hide again, the voice spoke out once more, but not quite so loudly this time.

"Please don't be afraid," said the giant. "Because I am a giant, no one will speak or play with me. Everyone thinks because I am so big, that I will hurt them. But I won't, really I won't."

Well, at first, the villagers made sure that they didn't get too near the giant to find out if he was friendly or not.

But each day, the giant would sit on a small hill near the village, and each day, the children would stand and stare at him.

After a while, because the giant seemed so gentle, they began to climb on him. The giant loved this, and soon the children found that he was a very gentle giant and played with him every day.

In the end, everyone was pleased that Jack had chosen their village to live near, as he kept the children happy.

Jack the gentle giant was happy too, now he was lonely no more.

Fun in Toyland

1. Tommy the toy soldier and his brother, Timothy, live in Toyland. Now, Timothy can be a rather mischievous boy and one day he did something rather naughty. He made a slide in the garden. Tommy slipped over on it.

2. "That was very naughty, Timothy," said Tommy. "I might have hurt myself on that slippery slide." Timothy was sorry. "I will put some salt on it," he said. Timothy knew salt would melt the ice on the path.

3. Tommy forgave his brother, and then went off to the palace to guard the King of Toyland. When he came home later, on his horse, Beauty, he saw furniture in the garden. "What now?" he thought.

4. Tommy soon found out what had happened. "I put the furniture outside, so that I could polish the floor for you," grinned Timothy. But seeing the way he did it Tommy knew he was really skating.

on a winter's day

5. Anyway, the floor looked nice and shiny, so Tommy helped Timothy to put the furniture back. Later on, Timothy asked Tommy if he could play on his sledge. "No," said Tommy. "It is dark outside."

6. At first Timothy was disappointed, but he knew Tommy was right. Then as he passed the stairs, he had one of his clever ideas. "I know where I can ride my sledge," he thought, "where it isn't dark."

7. Timothy got Tommy's toolbox and then pulled up the stair carpet. Then he nailed it down again so that it went straight up the stairs, like a hill. "Now I have a nice slope to slide down," he smiled.

8. By the time Tommy came out to find out what all the hammering was about, Timothy was having a sledge ride. "Whee, look at me!" he laughed. Tommy was too surprised to say anything. Naughty Timothy!

Old Mother Hubbard

Old Mother Hubbard
Went to the cupboard,

To fetch her poor dog a bone;
But when she came there

1. One day, Old Mother Hubbard went to her cupboard to get her dog some food. But there was nothing in the cupboard. "I am sorry, Rob," she said to her dog. "I have nothing for you to eat, and no money either."

2. Rob, Old Mother Hubbard's dog, decided to go and get food for himself. He came to where a man was playing an organ in the street. "I will dance for you," woofed Rob. Soon lots of folk came to watch the dog.

3. They thought he was clever and threw money into the man's hat. "I will soon have money to buy food," thought Rob. But he was wrong. The man finished playing, picked up his money and hat and went off.

4. The man had thought that Rob was just playing. He didn't know he was hungry. Then Rob saw some huge sausages hanging outside a shop. "One of those would be nice," he thought. When he bit one it burst.

and her poor dog

The cupboard was bare
And so the poor dog had none.

Now you can read the story below. It is about Old Mother Hubbard and her dog.

5. Rob had bitten a balloon! Frightened, Rob scampered away. It didn't seem as if he was ever going to get food. But then as he passed a butcher's shop, a kind butcher came out and threw him a juicy bone.

6. The dog picked up the bone and trotted home with it. Mother Hubbard was pleased to see her dog had something to eat. Rob lay in the garden chewing the bone for a while, then he decided to bury it to keep.

7. Mother Hubbard usually doesn't like Rob burying his bones, he makes such a mess. But this time she was delighted. Rob dug a hole in the garden and uncovered some coins someone had buried there long, long ago.

8. "You clever dog, Rob," she gasped. "Now I can go and buy us some nice food." She hurried off to the shop and was soon back with lots to eat. "Yum, yum," thought Rob. "Our cupboard will never be bare again."

COUNTRYSIDE

On these two pages are two countryside pictures for you to colour with your paints, crayons or colouring pencils. The first picture is of a man ploughing a field, as it was done many, many years ago before there were tractors.

COLOURING

The second picture is of a dear little robin perched on a fence-post on a winter's day. But before you start colouring, try and find three old-fashioned ploughs hidden in the first picture and three feathers hidden in the second picture.

Meet Teddy

1. Teddy Bear lives in Bear Green with his mummy and daddy and lots of other bears. One day, Teddy was riding his tricycle outside when he saw some Bear Scouts coming towards him, pulling a trolley.

2. "Hello, Teddy," said the Bear Scouts. "We are collecting things for our jumble sale. Have you got anything you don't want that we could take?" "Oh, yes," said Teddy. And he ran indoors as quickly as he could.

3. Mummy had already sorted out some things as she knew the Scouts would be coming. She had just given the things to the bears, when Teddy came running out with an old toy engine. "You can take this," he said.

4. "Thank you very much, you are kind," said a Scout. Then off they went to collect some more things. Later on, Mummy saw Teddy sitting sadly beside his toy cupboard. "I wish I hadn't given my engine," he sighed.

BOOKWORM DADDY HILL BILLY IVAN BEAR HONEY

Bear and his family

5. Mummy felt sorry for Teddy. He had been given that toy when he was a baby bear, and Mummy knew that now he was missing it. Just then there was a call from outside. When they looked out they saw Grandma.

6. "I have been to the Scouts' jumble sale," she said. "I have bought something for you both." Teddy and Mummy went downstairs. "Close your eyes, Teddy," said Grandma, holding something behind her back.

7. Teddy closed his eyes. Then Grandma said, "Open them now." What a lovely surprise Teddy had when he saw what Grandma had bought. She had bought his toy engine. "Thank you," he said.

8. "It is the loveliest present I have ever had," went on Teddy. Grandma was surprised. But Mummy explained. Then Grandma gave her a present—it was the scarf that Mummy had given to the Scouts!

The Three

1

Sing "Rub-a-dub-dub"
as three men in a tub
Are happily sailing the sea:
The Butcher, the Baker,
The Candlestick-maker,
Amounting—by counting—to three.

2

It's seven o'clock,
and they're due for a shock
For Willie the Whale is about.
They find themselves rising—
Which isn't surprising:
For they've all gone up on the spout!

The Whale's unaware
the sailors are there,
As long as his water spout blows.
But now it is stopping
And the bath tub is dropping
To land with a bump on his nose.

3

Now Willie is vexed
and what will he do next?
The sailors don't relish the thought.
They're paddling madly—
Discovering sadly
Their anchor's apparently caught.

Men in a Tub

4
But Willie the Whale,
with a flick of his tail
Is sending the tub on a trip.
The anchor is showing
The chest they've been towing
As all of them head for a ship.

5
They land on the deck,
and their tub is a wreck.
The Captain is pleased
with them though:
For he had discovered
The chest they've recovered
Is one that he lost long ago.

"For finding my chest,
you can take the crow's nest—
At least if you want it," he cries.
"Your tub, when it's mended,
For us will be splendid—
They're both of a similar size."

6
The Butcher says, "Please"
and the Baker agrees,
The Candlestick-maker, as well.
And as they head shoreward,
They're all looking forward
To home and the tale they will tell.

Keeping Harold's car warm

1. "What are you doing?" Harold asked his friend Happy Hedgehog. "Making sure that my car is nice and warm during the winter," said Happy. Harold was worried at that.

2. "Oh, my goodness," he gasped. "I haven't done anything to keep Buttercup warm." Buttercup is Harold's car! So grabbing Dicky's hand, Harold raced home very fast.

3. "We mustn't let Buttercup get cold in the winter, must we, Dicky?" said Harold. He ran indoors and took the bedclothes off the bed, and the electric fire from the bedroom.

4. He took the bedclothes to the garage, and carefully wrapped them round Buttercup. "Here is a hot water bottle too," said Harold, after he had turned on the electric fire.

5. "This is silly, Harold," said Dicky. But Harold took no notice. But that night, as he and Dicky sat shivering in bed, Harold realised that he had been a silly hare.

6. Then he had a simply brilliant idea. "Come downstairs, Dicky," he said. "It won't be any warmer down there," grumbled Dicky. But Harold ran out into the garden.

7. A few moments later, the funny hare was driving back into the lounge with Buttercup. "We can keep Buttercup warm and ourselves warm at the same time," said Harold.

8. Dicky was puzzled. "Come on Dicky," said Harold. "Get into the car with me, it is just like a bed." Harold was right. He, Dicky and Buttercup were all nice and warm!

HAROLD AND DICKY'S FUNNY RIDDLES:

Why is the sky like a hat?
Because it is always overhead.

What box has no lid?
A pillar box.

Which tree sounds sticky?
The gum-tree.

Where do snowmen dance?
At a snowball.

What lion never roars?
A dandelion.

What bulbs never grow?
Electric light bulbs.

The Engine that got tired of being an Engine

1. Eric the Engine was bored. "I am fed up with being an engine," he said. "Tired of always going along the same old lines and pulling the same old carriages." The naughty engine decided that he wanted to be something more exciting. So without being seen Eric got off his railway lines.

2. Soon he was chugging off in search of adventure. The first thing he met was a dodgem car. "Is it fun being a dodgem car?" he asked the dodgem car.

3. "Oh, yes," grinned the dodgem car. "It is fun. You race around bumping into each other. I can't think of anything more exciting than being a dodgem car." So Eric decided he would like to be a dodgem car. But he didn't like being bumped by the dodgem cars!

4. "Ouch, Ooo! Oh!" he gasped. "I don't like this at all." So he went off to find something else to be instead of a dodgem car. Soon he met Whizzy the rocket. "Is it fun being a rocket?" he asked Whizzy.
"Yes it is," said Whizzy.

5. "I race along as fast as I can and then fly into the air," said Whizzy. Eric decided he would like to be a rocket. Soon he and Whizzy were racing along side by side.

6. WHOOSH! Up into the air went Whizzy. But Eric stayed firmly on the ground. "I can't stop," he gasped. "I am going much too fast."

7. Suddenly the engine burst through a bush and landed—plonk—right on his very own railway lines again.

8. Suddenly Eric realised what it was that he really enjoyed doing best—being an engine and giving folk rides. Soon the Toyland folk were being pulled around by Eric the happy engine.

Nurse Susan and Doctor David

A LET'S PRETEND STORY

1. Nurse Susan and Doctor David are sister and brother who have their own Toys Hospital. One day, Susan and David were tidying the medicine cupboard. "Find some toys," Susan told the dolls.

2. So the dolly patients went to the toy cupboard and sorted out some toys to play with. "Look at Johnny Dolly," said the bear. Naughty Johnny had found a toy bow and arrow to play with.

3. Using his feet to hold the bow, Johnny pulled back the string and shot a rubber-tipped arrow. PLOP! The arrow landed on Susan's leg and stuck there. "Ooops," went Susan. It didn't hurt.

4. Johnny Dolly was very sorry. "Go and get Doctor David," said Susan. "He will know what to do." Soon David was there. He carefully pulled the arrow off Susan's leg—PERLOP!

5. "Oh, look," said Susan. "That sucker has left a red mark." "It needs some talcum powder dabbed on it," said David. "I will do it," said Johnny. Very carefully he dabbed on the powder.

6. Soon the red mark had vanished and Susan carried on with her work. "I think I will take this bow and arrow away," said David. "Yes," said Susan. So the dolls played with a roly toy.

The Lonely Little Elephant

IN the jungle there lived an elephant named Sam. He wasn't a great big elephant like the other elephants in the jungle. He was only a little elephant. And because he was only a little elephant, he was lonely.

All the other elephants used to laugh at him and call him 'shorty' and other horrid names.

Poor Sam, it seemed that he was all alone in the jungle, and didn't have any friends.

But Sam did have friends, only he didn't know it.

You see, also living in the jungle was a ladybird named Leonard. Leonard lived in a tree—a tree that talked. Theodor, the tree called himself.

These two had noticed that Sam was always alone, no one played with him, and no one spoke to him.

So they decided to do something about it.

One day, just as Sam was going past, the tree called out: "Hallo there, little elephant."

Sam stopped and stared. But he couldn't see anyone.

Then the voice said, "It is me, the tree, I can talk."

Little Sam was completely, totally, absolutely, amazed.

Then a little voice said: "My name is Leonard. We want to be your friends. But we want you to promise not to eat any of the leaves from my tree's branches."

Sam looked up at the juicy green leaves, that elephants love to eat.

"I promise," he said.

And Sam kept his promise.

The little elephant had found two friends and was lonely no more.

THE WOMBLES

On Wimbledon Common are some creatures called the Wombles. They go round making sure that the common is kept nice and tidy. The oldest and wisest Womble is Great Uncle Bulgaria. Madame Cholet is the Womble cook and Tobermory mends any of the bits and pieces the young Wombles find, in his workshop. Every day, the young Wombles, Tomsk, Wellington, Bungo and Orinoco go out wombling—picking up litter. Wombles are very shy creatures and don't like humans to see them.

Now, the laziest Womble is Orinoco. He would rather sleep than womble. So when he found an old washing basket, he thought, "Ah, a nice comfy place to have a rest." When Bungo and Wellington came along they found him fast asleep in the basket. "Let's teach Orinoco a lesson," said Bungo. "These balloons should do the trick." So they tied some balloons to the handles of the basket, thinking they would just make the basket and sleepy Orinoco float a little way above the ground. But look!

The balloons were rather large, and suddenly the basket rose into the air, higher and higher. "Ho, hum," yawned Orinoco, opening an eye. "I feel as if I am floating."

Then he looked down and found that he *was* floating—high in the sky. But luckily, the balloons got tangled in a tree. Just then along came Tomsk with a rope.

Bungo and Wellington explained what had happened. "I will soon rescue Orinoco," said Tomsk, making a lasso out of the rope. Then he started twirling it round his head.

"Hold out your arm, Orinoco," called Tomsk. So Orinoco did. Tomsk threw the lasso and the loop went round Orinoco's arm. "Now hold on," said Tomsk, and tugged.

The rope tightened round Orinoco's wrist and then Tomsk towed him in his basket back to the burrow. Great Uncle Bulgaria was surprised, but he was also quite pleased.

"That will make a nice place for me to rest," said Great Uncle Bulgaria. So Tobermory made a rope ladder and lots of cushions were put in. Lucky Great Uncle Bulgaria.

Nutty Noddle
THE FUNNY SQUIRREL

1. Nutty Noddle is a funny squirrel who lives in Nuttyville. One day, after he had bought a roll of carpet, Nutty saw his friend, Oswald Owl, looking at a notice. "It is the Nuttyville boat race today," said Oswald. "Will you come and watch it with me?"

2. "Ooo, yes," said Nutty. "I would love to watch the boat race. I can lay this stair carpet another day." So carrying the carpet and a hammer and nails, Nutty went with Oswald to the river to watch the race.

3. But when they got to the river, Nutty and Oswald found that lots of folk had got there before them. "Oh dear," said Oswald, "I cannot see the river at all, there are so many folk standing here already."

4. The friends were disappointed. "I was looking forward to seeing the race," said Oswald. Then Nutty had one of his nutty ideas. "Hold this carpet for me," he told Oswald. And then he started to climb a tree.

5. When he was sitting on a branch, he asked Oswald to pass up one end of the carpet to him and his hammer and nails. Then he started to nail that end of the carpet to the tree. "We will see the race," he said.

6. When Nutty had done that, he called the river patrol boat over. "Take us to the other side of the river, please," he said. As they went across the river, Oswald let the carpet unroll itself. Can you guess why?

7. On the other side of the river was another tree. Nutty nailed the other end of the carpet to this tree. So now the carpet stretched right across the river. "Come up here now, Oswald," said Nutty.

8. Nutty and Oswald crawled along the carpet until they were sitting in the middle. "Now we can watch the race easily," said Nutty. He was right about that. "Sometimes your nutty ideas are quite clever," grinned Oswald.

THE PRINCE AND THE BABY DRAGON

1. Once upon a time in the far away land of the Misty Moon, there lived a King and Queen. How pleased they were when a baby Prince was born to them. But the King's brother, Chang, wasn't so pleased. But for the new-born child he would be heir to the throne. So one night he crept into the nursery and tied a rope to the baby's cradle.

2. Then he lowered the cradle to a fast running river that ran beside the palace. "No child will rob me of the power I have wanted so long," thought Chang, as he watched the cradle being swept away down the river, soon to vanish from sight. On and on floated the cradle far away to another land.

3. Even though the river was rough, the cradle did not sink, and the baby slept all through his long journey. By morning, the cradle had been swept miles and miles from the palace. A fisherman caught the cradle in his net.

4. The fisherman's name was Lee and he and his wife had always wished for a baby of their own. It seemed that the wish had been granted when Lee saw the sleeping baby in the cradle. "Look what the river has brought us, Ming," he said to his wife, as he arrived home. How delighted the couple were.

5. So Lee and Ming decided to keep the baby as their own and they named him Wee Wong. As the years passed Wee Wong grew and grew. During this time the King died and the wicked Chang took his place. The Queen was made a prisoner in the palace. Often she would gaze out and wonder about her son.

6. Then one night, the Queen had a dream in which a voice told her that the river had taken her baby son. She told a wise man about her dream. He gave her a large egg, and said, "Place this egg in a cradle and lower it to the river. It is a magic egg and it will find your son." So that night the Queen did as she was told.

7. The egg floated down the river and soon disappeared from sight. On and on it floated until it came to where the baby Prince had been found. Then it got caught up in some reeds. One day, Wee Wong was playing near the river and found the egg! The magic had worked—but what sort of magic egg had the Prince found?

Continued on the next page . . .

8. At first Wee Wong thought that the egg belonged to some swans. So he picked it up and put it in their nest. The swans looked after the egg, as if it were their own. And then one day, the egg began to hatch. But it wasn't a baby swan that hatched from the egg—the strangest little creature that you ever saw came from the large egg. It was a baby dragon—a magical baby dragon.

9. When Wee Wong came to the river and saw the baby dragon he was very surprised. An even bigger suprise was in store for him. "Greetings, Wee Wong," said the dragon. "I have come to take you back to the land where you came from. For you are really a Prince, not a poor fisherman's son. Your wicked uncle now sits on your throne." Wee Wong took the dragon to Lee and Ming.

10. Lee and Ming were surprised when they saw Wee Wong approaching with a dragon. At first they were a bit frightened, but Wong said, "Do no be afraid. This dragon has come to tell you something." Then the dragon explained about Wee Wong being a Prince from another land. "His mother is missing him, and the new King is an evil man. So he must return with me."

11. Although Lee and Ming were upset at the thought of their son leaving them, they knew that they must let him go. So giving them a hug, Wee Wong said, "I will send for you." Then he climbed on to the back of the baby dragon and up up into the air he was carried. As he flew away, Wee Wong saw the village where he had lived for so long, disappearing in the distance, and he felt sad.

12. "Do not feel sad," said the dragon. "You will see Lee and Ming again." At last they came in sight of the palace in the land of the Misty Moon. The baby dragon flew straight to the part of the palace where the Queen was kept prisoner. "I have returned your son to you," said the dragon. "And he still wears the necklace you gave him as a baby." Sure enough the royal necklace hung round Wee Wong's neck. Then the Queen heard cheering below in the courtyard. The baby dragon had flown round telling folk that the Prince had been found. King Chang had been an unkind King and the people were glad that now he would have to leave. Wee Wong was crowned King of the land of the Misty Moon, and Lee and Ming came to live with him. King Wong ruled for many years, and he was a kind and thoughtful King and everyone in his land loved him and lived happily ever after.

Fliptail the Otter

1. One day, Fliptail was feeling bored. "I will go and see if Debbie will play with me," he thought. But when he went into Debbie's garden, he found her coming from the garden shed with a spade. "I'm busy," she said.

2. So Fliptail went back into Bramble Wood to see if he could find someone else to play with. Soon he met his friend, Robin. "Hallo, Robin," whistled Fliptail. "Will you play with me?" "Of course I will," chirped Robin.

3. Soon the two creatures were playing 'chase me' through the wood. Robin flew ahead of Fliptail, bobbing in the air, and Fliptail raced after him trying to touch him. Then they came to where Debbie was busy.

4. Debbie was busy digging up a little part of the garden that Daddy gave her to plant flowers in. Fliptail and Robin stood and watched. Suddenly something fell from Debbie's spade and rolled to Fliptail.

Fliptail the Otter lives in Bramble Wood with lots of other creatures. Near Bramble Wood is a pretty cottage and living in this cottage is a girl named Debbie. This little girl is a special friend of Fliptail's and he often goes to see her and they play together in the garden. Here is a story about them.

5. Fliptail sniffed it curiously. Then he picked it up in his paws and whistled at Debbie. The little girl turned to see what was wrong. "What have you got?" said Debbie, seeing that Fliptail was holding something.

6. Fliptail gave his find to Debbie. She took it indoors and washed off the dirt. "This is a coin of some sort," she told Mummy. It was so dirty, Debbie had to polish it. "Look, ten pence," gasped Debbie.

7. "Daddy must have dropped it," said Mummy. "I am sure he won't mind if you keep it." So Debbie took the coin and went to the toy shop. There she bought a lovely blue ball. Fliptail was excited when he saw it.

8. He knows that Debbie likes playing ball with him. "I hope that ball is for me," he thought. It *was!* "This is a present for you, Fliptail," said Debbie. "After all, you did find the coin." What a fine game the otter had!

Princess in the Tower

1. Long, long ago a wicked witch took away a Princess and locked her in the top of a tower to be her servant. Now the strange thing about the tower was that it had no stairs. But the witch could reach the top.

2. All she had to say was, "Rope of Gold" and the Princess lowered her long golden hair from the window. One day, a Prince was passing and heard and saw what the wicked old witch did. He was very puzzled.

3. "I must find out what is going on," he thought. He chose a moment when the witch was away, and then said the magic words. Down came the long golden hair, and the Prince climbed up. The Princess was afraid.

4. "You must go away, or that wicked old woman will keep you as a prisoner too," she said. "You cannot help me, there is no way for me to get down from this tower." But the Prince had fallen in love with the Princess.

5. He decided to get a ladder. So he hurried away. But, alas, the witch had spotted him. In a rage she went up into the tower using the golden hair, and then cut off the girl's long hair. "We will stay here for ever," she said.

6. But the wicked witch had forgotten one important thing to take with her when she went to her room to rest—the hair which she had cut off. Later the Princess used the hair to climb from the tower herself.

7. At the bottom of the tower the Prince was waiting. "I could not find a ladder long enough," he said. "But you seem to have found a way to escape." As they rode off they heard cries of rage from the witch.

8. The Princess was taken back to her father. The King was overjoyed to see his daughter back again. "Please may I marry this gallant Prince?" she asked. "Of course," said the King. "He saved you from the witch."

THE TOYMAKER

1. Once upon a time there was a travelling toymaker. He travelled from town to town making toys for children who wanted them. But in one town, the mayor came up and told the toymaker to go away. ''Be off,'' he said.

2. ''Children should be in school, not watching you,'' said the mayor, as the toymaker left the town. Outside the town the toymaker sat down sadly. He knew the children were upset. The toys were sad, too.

3. ''If we don't help the toymaker go back to that town, we won't have nice homes to live in,'' said one of the toys. ''Nor will we have children to play with us,'' said another toy. So they decided to help the toymaker.

4. Just look what they did. All the toys marched back to the town, leaving the toymaker resting by his cart. ''We will soon teach that nasty mayor a lesson,'' said the cowboy toy. On they marched into town.

AND THE TOYS

5. Then, that night, when everyone was asleep, those toys went to every house in the town to get more help. They climbed through windows, over walls and crept in through doors, making sure that no one heard them.

6. In each and every house, the toys went to the toy cupboards and called to the other toys that were there, "Come and help us teach the wicked mayor of this town a lesson." All the toys were ready to help.

7. They all went to the mayor's house and made a terrible lot of noise, calling him a horrid man, and booing him, until the mayor could stand it no more. He ran to the toymaker. "Please come back," he said.

8. The toymaker was most surprised. But he went back to the town, and the toys went back to their homes. Then the children came out and chose toys from the toymaker. How happy the toymaker was—thanks to the toys!

Katie Country Mouse

1. Aunt Matilda had come to stay with Katie Country Mouse. One day, Katie said, "Let's go and see Theresa Mouse." Matilda said she would like to do that. So off they set to Theresa's house.

2. "Theresa lives on the other side of Dimble Stream," said Katie. "We shall have to cross on a bullrush to get to the other side." Matilda watched as Katie trotted across a bullrush.

3. Now, Matilda was a Town Mouse, and she had never crossed a stream on a bullrush before. She got on the stem and then wobbled her way along it. "Oh, oh," she gasped. "I am slipping."

4. Katie gasped, as Matilda fell off the bullrush. Plonk! She landed right on the back of Thomas Frog. "Oh dear, I am sorry," said Matilda. "Don't worry," said Thomas, and he leaped into the air.

5. Matilda held on tight as Thomas landed on the other side of the stream. "There you are," he said. "That is an easier way to cross." Matilda thanked and they went to have tea with Theresa.

6. Theresa couldn't help smiling when she heard about Matilda's adventure. They sat chatting for quite a while, until it was night and time to go home. This time Katie went a different way home.

Four Puzzling Puzzles

1 Which path do the boy and his daddy have to take to reach the football match?

2 Join the dots with a pencil to see something that lives in the sea.

3 Put the first letter of each object's name in the circle beneath it to see what grows on an oak tree.

4 Which prize cup is different from the others?

ANSWERS:

(1) Path a (2) You drew an octopus. (3) ACORN: A-rrow, C-arrot, O-wl, R-ake, N-est. (4) Cup C has different handles.

The Dancing Shoes

1. Once there was a girl named Kay. Her mother sent her to buy new shoes. As she went into the shoe shop she saw some red dancing shoes. Kay decided that she would try them on.

2. The red dancing shoes fitted perfectly, and although they were not what her mother had sent her to buy, she bought them. "They are special dancing shoes as you will find out," said the man.

3. As Kay went home, she passed a man playing a music box. A pretty dancing tune was coming from the box, and suddenly, Kay found herself dancing beautifully to the pretty tune.

4. Round and round she danced. "I have never danced like this before," thought Kay. "It must be these special shoes." Soon lots of folk were watching her and putting money in the man's hat.

5. Then Kay noticed it was nearly tea time. "I must go home," she thought. But do you know something, Kay didn't walk home—she danced. The shoes would not stop dancing!

6. "Oh dear, I wish they would stop," puffed Kay, who was getting quite tired. At last she managed to untie the ribbons on the shoes, and the shoes went dancing away into the woods.

7. On and on danced the shoes, leaving Kay feeling rather worried. "I have wasted the money mother gave me to buy some shoes," she sighed. Then the old man with the music box hurried up.

8. "If it hadn't been for your beautiful dancing, people would not have given me so much money," he said. And he gave some to Kay—enough for her to buy new shoes. Lucky girl.

WINK AND BLINK TWO PLAYFUL LITTLE PUPPIES

Wink and her brother, Blink, like to play ball together. So you can imagine how they felt, when they found that the box that Blink kept his ball in was empty. "I am sure I put it here after I had played with it last time," said Blink. Anyway, the two puppies decided to search for the missing ball. They searched in their kennel and even in a flower pot for their ball. Funny pups!

But it could not be found anywhere. "Where can it be?" grumbled Wink. "I am sure you must have lost it, Blink." Blink looked quite hurt. "I am sure I put it back in its box," he said. "Maybe we can find another one." So the pups went to search for a new ball. As they were walking down a street, Blink spotted a black ball. "That will do," he said.

But he hadn't found a ball, had he? "Let's take it home," said Wink. So Blink picked up the ball very gently in his mouth and carried it home. Neither he, nor Wink noticed that this ball had a tube on it, and on the end of the tube was a flower—a joke flower! Back home, Blink said, "I am going to give this ball a big bite." Then Wink saw the flower and sniffed it.

Oh dear. Just look what happened. The black ball-shaped thing was full of water, and as Blink bit it, the water was swooshed along the tube to the flower. WHOOSH! The water came squirting out of the flower and went straight into Wink's face. "Who did that?" she gasped. Blink turned and looked. "I think it was me," he thought. "And I don't think Wink will be pleased."

Blink was right about that. Wink was not at all pleased. In fact she was *very* cross. "You naughty, naughty pup," she scolded. "Come here and I will squirt water over you." "It was a mistake, really it was," wuffed Blink, as he scampered away from angry Wink. Ahead of him, Blink saw a hole. He decided that he would hide down it, until Wink had cheered up.

That hole led to where Mrs. Rabbit and her babies lived. And in their home was a striped ball, just like the one Wink and Blink had lost. "That is our ball," gasped Blink. "Oh, is it?" said Mrs. Rabbit. "We were wondering who it belonged to. It rolled down here the other day." It was then that Blink remembered that he *had* lost the ball. Silly Blink.

Blink thanked Mrs. Rabbit, picked up the ball in his mouth, and wriggled out of the hole again. Wink was happy when she saw he had found the ball. "I forgive you for squirting me with water," she said. "I realise now that it was an accident." Blink gave her a loving lick, and then the two pups did what they liked doing best—they played ball. What fun those jolly little pups had.

Freddie Frog

FREDDIE Frog and his friend Terry Tortoise live in Bumble Down. One day, Montgomery Mole showed them a picture of himself on holiday. "Look at brave me," said Montgomery. "I stood as close as I could to those big elephants." When they got back home, Freddie told Terry that he wanted his picture taken with a wild animal. "I will show Montgomery what a brave frog I am," boasted Freddie. He put on his explorer's outfit and, taking his camera, went to the zoo with Terry. He told the zoo keeper that he wanted his picture taken standing beside a large animal. "You can stand next to Adolf," said the keeper. Adolf was a huge fierce-looking ox. "Er, couldn't you find me something a little bit smaller to stand next to?" asked Freddie nervously, as Adolf glared at him.

and the picture

"Of course I could," said the zoo keeper. He took Freddie and Terry to the part of the zoo where the children's pets were kept. "Jenny the gazelle is very gentle," said the keeper, as he led a rather sweet little gazelle over to Freddie. But as soon as the keeper let go of Jenny, she started to prance about. Freddie ran away as quickly as he could. "Don't worry," said the keeper. "She only wants to play." But Freddie was too scared to listen. "I don't think I will bother with a picture after all," he sighed. But as he and Terry were leaving the zoo, they saw a poster with the picture of a fierce lion on it. So Freddie decided to have his picture taken standing beside the poster. "It will look as if I am feeding this lion, won't it?" said Freddie. And it did! Naughty Freddie Frog.

The Little Mermaid

ONCE upon a time there was a little mermaid named Pearl. She lived at the bottom of the deep blue sea in a pretty little coral cave. Beautiful sea anemones grew outside her cave and she looked after them and kept her home nice and tidy.

But although Pearl had a lovely home and had lots of nice friends, she was a very discontented mermaid.

Pearl knew that on the edge of the sea there was a place the sea folk called The Land.

She longed to see what The Land looked like, and begged many of her friends to take her to see it.

"Please take me to The Land on your back," she begged Paul Porpoise.

"No, no!" said Paul. "The land is no place for a little mermaid. You stay here."

Pearl went home and sat outside her cave looking quite sad.

Just then along came two of her seahorse friends, Sam and Samantha.

"Why are you looking so glum?" Sam asked.

"It isn't like you to be sad," said Samantha. "Please tell us what is wrong."

Pearl explained that she wanted to see what The Land was like.

"I don't want to go on to it," she said, "just see what it looks like."

Sam and Samantha looked a bit worried when they heard that.

"The Land isn't very nice," they said. "We are glad that we live under the sea. You should be pleased too."

"But I don't *know* that," said Pearl. "After all I have *never* seen The Land."

So the two seahorses said they would take Pearl and show her The Land.

So using a large seashell as a carriage, Pearl was taken to see The Land by the seahorses.

On they went, until the sea started to get shallower.

"We are nearly there," said Sam, as they floated to the top of the sea.

Suddenly Pearl found herself floating on top of the sea on her shell, and ahead of her was a strange sight.

There was a sort of golden colour near the sea, leading up to some white tall things topped with lovely green colour with funny-shaped things on them.

What Pearl could see was the beach, the cliffs, the grass and some houses.

But suddenly a big wave came rolling along, and Pearl found her shell being swooshed on to the shore and into a rocky pool.

Then a loud voice said, "Ooo, Mummy, look at this pretty shell."

Pearl quickly hid inside her shell as it was lifted out of the pool.

A little girl named Sue had found the shell, and she took it with her and put it on a cupboard in her bedroom.

It seemed that Pearl would never see her home under the sea again, and that night she began to cry, "I wish I hadn't wanted to see The Land so much."

Now, it just happened that Sue heard the mermaid crying.

"Who is there?" she said. "Please come out. I won't hurt you."

Pearl peeked out. Sue was amazed, and the mermaid explained what had happened.

"It is my own fault really," she said.

Kind Sue told her not to worry. "I will take you back to the sea in the morning," she told Pearl.

And that is just what she did.

Soon the mermaid was swimming in the sea, and back to where Sam and Samantha were waiting for her.

"You were right," she told them as they took her home. "It is much nicer under the sea in my own little home."

And that is where she lived happily ever after.

Tiger Tim
and the Bruin Boys

1. It was Drawing Lesson time at Mrs. Bruin's school, and Tiger Tim and the Bruin Boys were trying to draw Jumbo. "Try and do some life-like pictures of Jumbo and each other," said Mrs Bruin, as she left to get tea.

2. The pictures weren't very life-like, were they? Then Bobby decided to shine a lamp at Jumbo. "That is clearer," he said. "Just look at that lovely sharp shadow of Jumbo on the wall," said Tiger Tim excitedly.

3. That shadow gave Tim and Jacko a good idea—it was a naughty one really. "Jumbo's shadow is the same shape as Jumbo," said Tim. So he drew round the shadow, and Jacko filled in the shadow with ink.

4. "Mrs. Bruin will be pleased with our picture, Tim," giggled Jacko. "Yes, it looks very life-like." So next Tim did a picture of Bobby—in red ink. "My turn next," said Fido the dog. "I will paint Joey."

5. Well, it wasn't long before those naughty boys had made ink shadow pictures on the wall of them all. Tim was right, the shadow pictures did look very life-like. But when Mrs. Bruin came in she wasn't very pleased.

6. "What have you done?" she gasped. Tim explained that they had done just what she had asked them to do. "Our pictures do look life-like, don't they?" he said. "Bring your pencils into the kitchen," said Mrs. Bruin.

7. The boys found their pencils and then went to the kitchen. They were pleased when they saw a big cake on the table. "Goody! Tea-time," laughed Tim. "Take your seats at the table," said Mrs. Bruin. "Hurry up."

8. The boys didn't need to be told to hurry. They were soon sitting at the table, then they had a shock. "Before tea, you can all do a life-like picture of my cake," she said. "Then you can have tea, *after* cleaning the wall!"

1. It was a snowy Christmas day in Toyland and Tommy and Dolly were going to have a Christmas tree party. As they were pulling the tree home, Bouncer Ball came bouncing up.

2. "I am looking forward to your party," he said. "I have been bouncing around all day waiting for the time to pass." Tommy and Dolly went to get the decorations.

3. While they were away, Gerald Giraffe came by. Like all giraffes, he is very fond of eating leafy things. So when he saw the little tree, he licked his lips.

4. "Yum, yum," thought Gerald. "That tree looks very tasty indeed." And before you could say *Gerald the greedy giraffe,* he was munching up that lovely little Christmas tree.

in Toyland

5. By the time Tommy and Dolly came out with the decorations, Gerald had eaten all the green branches. "You naughty giraffe," said Dolly. "You have spoilt our party."

6. Of course Gerald hadn't meant to spoil anything. But it was too late to get another tree. So do you know what Tommy did? He started hanging the decorations on to Gerald.

7. "Gerald can be our tree," he said. And when Tommy had finished, Gerald looked very nice indeed. And the folk of Toyland had a very nice Christmas tree party after all.

Jack and Jill's Puzzles

1

Can you show Little Bo-Peep the way through this maze to reach her little lamb. Does she have to take path 1, 2 or 3?

2

The two pictures below seem the same. But the artist has made five big changes in the picture B. Can you see those changes?

3

With a pencil join the dots from number 1 to number 23 to see something that flies.

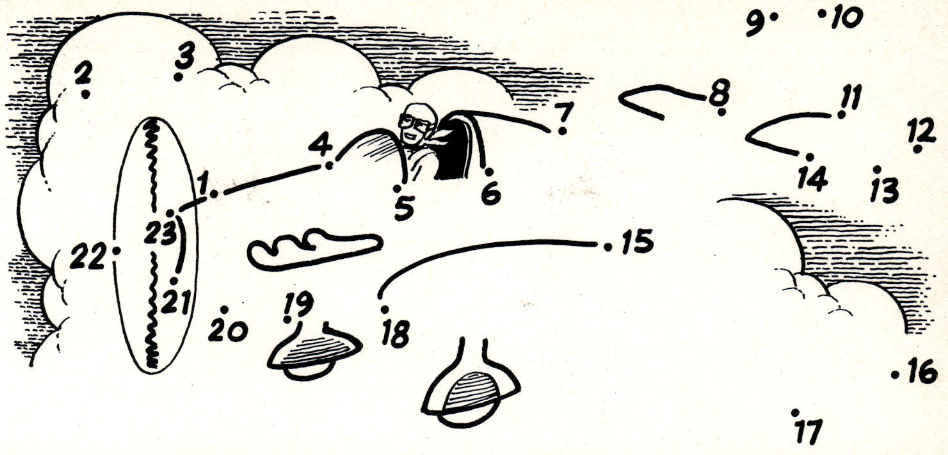

4

Try and pair up the letters with the objects. Do this by saying out loud what they are and pair ones that rhyme, like: B and key.

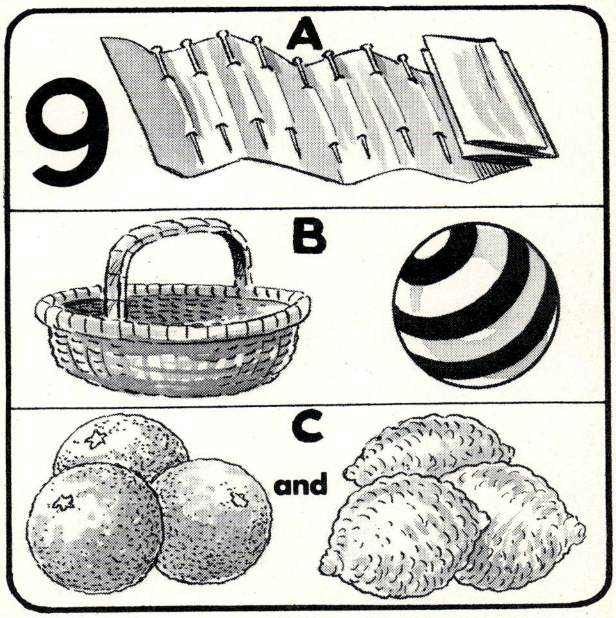

5

Say the names of the pairs of objects and put the names together to name three games that are fun to play.

ANSWERS:

(1) Path 2 led to the lamb. (2) The changes made were 1. The birds in the sky have been moved. 2. The clouds are different. 3. The path is straighter. 4. The window on the windmill has been moved. 5. A door is wider. (3) You drew an aeroplane. (4) The other pairs were: L - bell, N - pen, O - bow, U - shoe, R - star and Y - tie. (5) The games were: A. nine-pins, B. basket-ball, C. oranges and lemons. (6) The matching pairs were: 1 and 3, 2 and 5, 4 and 6.

6

Pair up these six jugs into three pairs that have matching patterns on them.

Snuggles the Koala Bear

Snuggles is a cuddly Koala Bear who lives on a farm with a little girl named Susan. Major the dog and Spitzi the Siamese cat also live on the farm. Although Snuggles is a dear little bear, he sometimes causes a bit of trouble, as you will see in this story.

1. One day, Snuggles saw Major balancing a biscuit on his nose. "Now you can eat that," said Susan. Snuggles smiled.

2. "If Major gets a treat for doing a clever trick, perhaps I can do the same," he thought. Now, Snuggles loves treacle. So he got a tin.

3. Then balancing the tin on his nose, he walked across the kitchen floor. "Susan is sure to let me have some," he thought.

4. But then the tin toppled off his nose—crash on to the floor. The lid came off and treacle spilt on the floor. Susan was cross.

5. "Now I shall have to clear it up," she said. "Naughty Snuggles!" The Koala knew how to clean up the treacle—he licked it up.

6. When Susan came back, the floor was clean. Susan was pleased. "Clever!" she said. "I enjoyed that," thought Snuggles.

GREGORY AND THE DORMICE

GREGORY Grasshopper met two little dormice one day. "When the farmer was cutting his corn, he cut our house down," they told Gregory. The kind grasshopper knew what to do. He went and found Willie Woodpecker. "These two mice need a new home," he told him. Willie was soon busy.

Using his strong beak, Willie pecked two holes in a hollow tree. When he had finished, the dormice had a lovely little home. "The farmer won't cut down this home," they said happily. "Thank you, Gregory. If there is anything we can do for you, please come and ask." Gregory said he would do that, and then he hopped on to Willie's back and the woodpecker flew off. "I will come and see you again," waved Gregory to his friends.

Willie took Gregory back to where he lived with the other insects. A little later on, Gregory found a toy farm set in a girl's garden. When he saw the toy cart, he had a simply splendid idea. He hurried back to the tree where the dormice were and spoke to one of them. "It would be nice if you could come and play with us," said Gregory. And he explained about the toy cart.

Gregory and the dormouse went to where the toy farm cart was. And then look what they did. The kind dormouse pulled the cart with Gregory and his friends in it round the garden. "This is fun," they said.

PRINCESS OF

1. Long, long ago a young nobleman was out riding in a forest. Suddenly he was startled by a shaft of bright golden light coming from the tree tops. "It cannot be sunlight," he thought, looking up at a large oak tree.

2. In the tree he saw a beautiful girl with golden hair. It was from her gleaming hair that the light was coming. The man asked the girl if she needed help. "No," said the girl. "I have always lived in this tree."

3. And she explained that when she was a baby, an eagle had taken her from her home and put her in the nest. "I am the Princess of the Eagles." "Please come down, so that I may marry you," called the young man.

4. "I will not do that unless you can *make* me leave this tree," said the girl. The young man rode away feeling very sad. Later he came to where a dwarf was making a fire. He explained about the girl in the tree.

THE EAGLES

5. "How can I make her come down" sighed the man. The dwarf smiled. "I know," he said. He took his cooking things to the tree.

6. Then he kept putting his cooking pot down in such a way that it kept tipping over. "Silly man," thought the girl. "I will have to help him."

7. She climbed down from the tree and showed him that he must stand the pot on level ground. "Oh, I see," said the dwarf, giving a big smile.

8. Then to the girl's amazement, the dwarf picked her up and ran off through the forest with her. The girl was too surprised to say anything, and the dwarf ran as fast as the swiftest deer. Soon he came to the man.

9. "There," said the dwarf. "I made the Princess of the Eagles come down from her nest for you." The young man smiled and took the girl's hand. "Will you marry me now?" he said. "Yes," said the girl "I will."

Gardening Trouble

1. The weather had been very hot, and it hadn't rained for a long time so the flowers in Nutty's garden looked thirsty. "I must give them a drink," decided Nutty. But that was hot work and Nutty wished he could play in his sand pit.

2. "There must be an easier way to water flowers," thought Nutty, as he went to fill his watering can once more. Then he saw a hose in the garden shed. "That is just what I need," smiled Nutty. So he got out the hose.

3. He connected it to the tap and then started to squirt water at the flowers. SWOOSH! The water came out of the hose very fast indeed. "Oh dear," sighed Nutty. "I think this is too strong for my flowers."

4. Poor Nutty, the watering can took too long, and the hose was too strong. But he knew that the flowers needed water. Then Nutty saw the washing line and had one of his ideas. "That's what I need," he thought.

5. So he took the washing line down from its posts. Then he went and got a ladder. "First I must tie this washing line to the drainpipe on my house," he decided. Soon he was doing just that. Can you guess why?

6. Then he took the other end of the line to a tree on the other side of the garden. When he had put the washing line through the handle of the watering can, he tied the line round the tree. He was pleased with himself.

7. When he had done that, he tied the end of the hose to the watering can so the nozzle pointed into it. "Now I can water the garden easily," he grinned. And below you can see how the funny squirrel managed to do that.

8. The washing line went over the flower bed, and as the hose filled up the can, water came sprinkling out over the flowers. Nutty tied a piece of string to the can, so that he could pull it along without leaving his sand pit. What a nutty idea. But it worked, didn't it?

ONCE UPON a time in a far away Eastern Land there lived a brave young prince named Fortuna. He had a young sister, Princess Marabella, who he loved very much. They were together nearly all the time and they loved to ride their horses across the wide plains of their land. All the people of the country loved the young prince and knew that when his time came, he would be a fair and kind ruler.

The Tears of Pearl

But Prince Fortuna had one enemy, his uncle Zarka, who wished to be the next ruler of the land. One day, the wicked uncle went to see a magician and offered him many riches as a reward if he would think of a way to get rid of the prince. The magician was only too pleased to help Zarka out. "But to cast a spell, I must get the prince to come to my cave," said the magician. He looked into his crystal ball to see how he could do this.

The crystal ball showed the magician that the prince often took his horse to a pool where he would let it drink after its long gallop across the plains. So that night, the magician made up a special potion and poured it in the pool. ''As soon as the prince's horse drinks from this pool,'' laughed the magician, ''it will gallop to my cave. Nothing will be able to stop it.'' Sure enough, the next day, the prince came riding up to the pool. He had been racing his sister, and had reached the pool first. His horse bent its head and started to drink from the pool. After its first sip, the horse suddenly flung up its head and went galloping away up the hill. The prince could not stop it, and the princess watched in dismay.

On and on galloped the horse until it came to the magician's cave.

Continued on the next page . . .

The wicked magician had been expecting Prince Fortuna and as the horse pulled up outside the cave he went out to greet him. The prince was tired and the magician invited him in. Inside the cave he offered the prince a magic apple. As soon as Fortuna took a bite from the apple, he changed into a gazelle. When that had happened, the magician shooed the gazelle from his cave, and the frightened creature rushed off to the plains. Zarka was delighted when the magician told him that the spell had worked. "The spell can only be broken if the gazelle eats tears that turn into pearls," the magician told him. "That will never happen," said Zarka. "Already my finest huntsmen are hunting for the gazelle."

But the gazelle realised that it was in great danger and mingled amongst some wild goats as the uncle's huntsmen roamed the plains searching for the gazelle. The gazelle knew that it must somehow reach the royal palace and find Princess Marabella. Each time it approached the palace, the gazelle heard the noise of galloping hooves and had to find a hiding place, only the speed of the gazelle kept it ahead of the hunters. But at last the bewitched prince managed to reach the palace and creep behind two guards as they stood talking. Up the stairs went the gazelle and into the princess's room. The poor creature was so tired that it lay down at the princess's feet. Princess Marabella did not know that the gazelle was really her missing brother. But she

felt very sorry for the poor, tired creature.

"Quickly, bring water for this beautiful creature," said the princess to one of her maids. The girl hurried away and was soon back with a bowl of fresh water. But alas, as she hurried to the princess's room, Zarka spotted her. "Why are you taking that water to the princess's room?" he asked. The girl told him about the gazelle. Later the uncle came into the princess's room. "That gazelle must not stay here," he said crossly. "His place is on the plains where he will provide sport for my huntsmen."

"You can't be so cruel," said the princess, but seeing her uncle's harsh face, she knew that he meant every word. Suddenly Marabella started to cry.

Continued on the next page . . .

As her tears fell on the floor they changed into pearls—the princess was crying tears of pearl. Seeing those tears made Zarka remember the magician's words. He tried to pick up the pearls, but there were too many. "The gazelle must not have them," he gasped. But he was too late. The gazelle bent its neck and picked up a tear of pearl in its mouth. As soon as the gazelle bit into the pearl, there was a flash, and it turned back into the prince again. Uncle Zarka gave a cry of dismay. Then he fled from the room, and out of the palace. He feared that the prince would be angry, and he galloped to the magician to try and get him to cast another magic spell.

The princess was overjoyed to see her brother again. "How did you become a gazelle?" she asked. The prince thought, and then he remembered where his horse had taken him after drinking from the pool. With some guards the prince went to the magician's cave and there he found his wicked uncle with the magician. "So it was you who tried to get rid of me," said the prince. Zarka begged for mercy and was told to leave the land, never to return again. As for the rest of the tears of pearl, these were made into a necklace for the princess, and she and the prince lived happily ever after.

THE END

Teddy's Exciting Dream

TEDDY Bear loves watching bands on television. He thinks that the person who plays the drums has the most exciting job. One night he had the most exciting dream. He dreamed that he was in a band playing the drums. Bangity-bang-bang, went Teddy playing as fast as he could. All the bears of Bear Green were watching him and they clapped when he had finished. "Well done, Teddy," they clapped. Teddy did feel proud. But then he woke up and found that it was only a dream. "Time for school," said Mummy. So Teddy went off to school. Well, at school, there is a band, and Teddy's teacher called Teddy to the front of the class and asked him if he would like to be in the band. Teddy was excited. "Yes, yes," he said. And guess what Teddy played in the school band? He played the drums. And what a good player he was as you can see. Teddy's dream had come true. Can you find four other instruments hidden above?

TOYS FOR YOU TO MAKE

On this page are some toys for you to make. You can trace the pictures if you don't want to spoil your book and then stick them on thin card.

First are two walk-along toys. Cut them out separately and cut out the white round pieces. Then put your fingers through the holes to act as legs.

On the left is a jigsaw for you to make. Cut out all the pieces separately and then try to fit them together to see Harold Hare and Dicky Dormouse swimming under the water with some fish.

Now you can make a toy of Dicky paddling a canoe. The pictures must be cut out first. Then slits are made along the paddle arm so that the arm of the paddle can be slipped over the figure of Dicky so that it goes in front of him. The green tab and Dicky's arms go behind the figure. Then when the tab is wiggled from side to side it will look as if Dicky is paddling his canoe.

The Lucky Bean

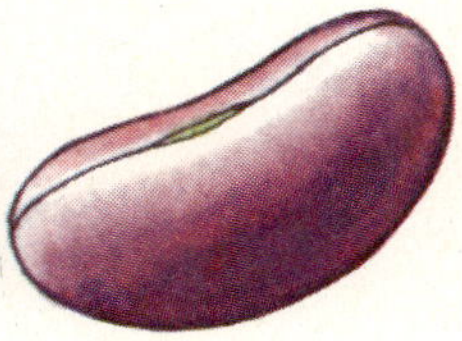

ONCE there was a bag of beans. An old woman bought these beans to cook for her tea. As she threw them into a pot of boiling water, one of them managed to miss the pot.

This bean landed beside a piece of straw and a piece of coal.

The Straw, the Coal and the Bean began to talk. "What good luck we have had," said the Coal."I and the Straw, haven't been burnt, and you, Bean haven't been cooked."

"Yes," said the Bean. "Let's travel together."

The Straw and the Coal agreed.

Soon they were wandering along a woodland path. But then they came to a stream.

"How shall we cross this stream?" said the Coal.

"You can use me as a bridge," said the Straw.

The Straw stretched itself across the stream. The Bean went first, and was soon on the other side.

But when the Coal started to cross it took its time, and the Straw called out, "Hurry, hurry."

But it was too late. The Straw snapped and both the Coal and the Straw fell into the stream.

The Bean giggled, which turned into a big laugh. He laughed so much that he split himself in two.

Luckily a kind tailor came along.

As carefully as he could, he stitched up the Bean.

"Thank you," said the Bean.

Now, the tailor had used black cotton, and that explains why every Bean has a black seam.

TOPSY-TURVY
YUMMY

1. Harold Hare and Dicky Dormouse were very busy in the kitchen. They were making an extra-special yummy stew. It was full of yummy carrots and many other things that Harold and Dicky love to eat. "It will soon be ready," said Harold.

2. "But just to make it extra-yummy," went on Harold. "I will put in some more carrots." Well, Harold was just laying the table when Dicky saw Uncle David Rabbit coming up the garden path. "Uncle David is coming," he called.

3. "Oh, no," gasped Harold. "He can't be coming, not now, not after all my cooking." "Quick, let's hide," said Dicky. So they did. You see, Uncle David is a very greedy rabbit, who loves to eat and eat and eat!

4. Harold and Dicky knew that if they let him in, they would have to share their stew with him, and that meant *he* would eat most of it! Uncle David came indoors. He didn't see Harold and Dicky. Can you see them hiding from him?